EMMANUEL JOSEPH

Threaded Days, Weaving Mindfulness, Productivity, and Relationships into Everyday Life

Copyright © 2025 by Emmanuel Joseph

All rights reserved. No part of this publication may be reproduced, stored or transmitted in any form or by any means, electronic, mechanical, photocopying, recording, scanning, or otherwise without written permission from the publisher. It is illegal to copy this book, post it to a website, or distribute it by any other means without permission.

First edition

This book was professionally typeset on Reedsy.
Find out more at reedsy.com

Contents

1	Chapter 1: The Art of Mindful Living	1
2	Chapter 2: Cultivating Productive Habits	3
3	Chapter 3: Nurturing Relationships	5
4	Chapter 4: Balancing Work and Life	7
5	Chapter 5: The Power of Positive Thinking	9
6	Chapter 6: Embracing Change and Adaptability	11
7	Chapter 7: Cultivating Creativity	13
8	Chapter 8: Building Resilience	15
9	Chapter 9: Enhancing Emotional Intelligence	17
10	Chapter 10: Practicing Mindful Eating	19
11	Chapter 11: Managing Stress and Anxiety	21
12	Chapter 12: Developing a Growth Mindset	23
13	Chapter 13: Enhancing Focus and Concentration	25
14	Chapter 14: Building Strong Support Networks	27
15	Chapter 15: Developing Time Management Skills	29
16	Chapter 16: Exploring Mindful Movement	31
17	Chapter 17: Creating a Mindful Home Environment	33

1

Chapter 1: The Art of Mindful Living

Mindfulness is the practice of being present in the moment, fully engaged with whatever we are doing. It's about cultivating an awareness that allows us to experience life more deeply and richly. When we live mindfully, we can appreciate the small joys and navigate the inevitable challenges with grace and resilience. Incorporating mindfulness into our daily routines helps us to stay centered and focused, leading to a more balanced and fulfilling life.

To begin our journey into mindfulness, it's essential to understand the power of breath. Our breath is a constant companion, always available to anchor us in the present moment. By paying attention to our breathing, we can calm our minds and reduce stress. Start with simple breathing exercises, such as taking a few deep breaths or practicing diaphragmatic breathing. Over time, these practices will become second nature, allowing us to maintain a sense of calm even in the midst of chaos.

Another crucial aspect of mindful living is cultivating gratitude. Gratitude helps us to shift our focus from what's lacking in our lives to what we already have. It encourages us to appreciate the abundance around us, fostering a sense of contentment and happiness. Begin each day by listing a few things you are grateful for, and make it a habit to express gratitude to others. This practice not only enhances our well-being but also strengthens our relationships.

Lastly, mindful living involves being fully present in our interactions with others. When we listen attentively and respond with empathy, we create deeper connections and more meaningful relationships. Practice active listening by giving your full attention to the person speaking, and avoid interrupting or planning your response while they are talking. By being present in our conversations, we can build trust and foster a greater sense of understanding.

2

Chapter 2: Cultivating Productive Habits

Productivity is not about doing more; it's about doing what matters most. To cultivate productive habits, we need to prioritize our tasks and focus on what truly adds value to our lives. This requires a shift in mindset, from simply being busy to being intentional with our time and energy. By adopting a more mindful approach to productivity, we can achieve our goals without sacrificing our well-being.

One of the most effective ways to boost productivity is to establish a daily routine. Routines provide structure and predictability, helping us to stay organized and focused. Start by creating a morning routine that sets a positive tone for the day, and follow it with a consistent schedule for work and personal activities. Include regular breaks to recharge and avoid burnout. A well-planned routine allows us to manage our time more efficiently and accomplish more with less effort.

Another key to productivity is setting clear and achievable goals. Break down larger projects into smaller, manageable tasks and set deadlines for each step. This approach makes it easier to track progress and stay motivated. Use tools such as to-do lists, calendars, and project management apps to stay organized and keep your goals in sight. Remember to celebrate your achievements, no matter how small, as this reinforces positive behavior and encourages continued progress.

Eliminating distractions is also essential for maintaining productivity.

Identify the factors that disrupt your focus and find ways to minimize or eliminate them. This may involve creating a dedicated workspace, turning off notifications, or setting boundaries with others. Practice single-tasking, where you focus on one task at a time, rather than multitasking. By reducing distractions and maintaining focus, you can work more efficiently and produce higher-quality results.

3

Chapter 3: Nurturing Relationships

Relationships are the cornerstone of a fulfilling life. They provide us with support, love, and a sense of belonging. Nurturing our relationships requires effort, time, and commitment. By practicing mindfulness and being present in our interactions, we can strengthen our connections and build more meaningful bonds with others.

Effective communication is the foundation of any healthy relationship. This involves not only speaking clearly and honestly but also listening actively and empathetically. When we communicate mindfully, we are more attuned to the needs and feelings of others, fostering greater understanding and trust. Practice expressing your thoughts and emotions openly, while also being receptive to the perspectives of those around you.

Another important aspect of nurturing relationships is showing appreciation and gratitude. Expressing gratitude helps to reinforce positive behaviors and strengthens the emotional bond between individuals. Make it a habit to acknowledge and appreciate the efforts and qualities of those around you. Whether it's a simple thank you or a heartfelt note, these gestures can have a profound impact on your relationships.

Spending quality time together is also crucial for nurturing relationships. In our busy lives, it's easy to become disconnected from those we care about. Make an effort to prioritize time with family and friends, engaging in activities that you enjoy together. This could be anything from sharing a meal to going on a hike or simply having a meaningful conversation. The key is to be fully present and attentive during these moments, fostering a deeper connection and sense of closeness.

Finally, it's important to practice forgiveness and understanding in our relationships. Conflicts and misunderstandings are inevitable, but how we handle them can make all the difference. Approach disagreements with a mindset of empathy and compassion, seeking to understand the other person's perspective. Be willing to apologize and forgive, as holding onto grudges can damage relationships. By practicing forgiveness, we create space for healing and growth, allowing our relationships to thrive.

4

Chapter 4: Balancing Work and Life

Finding a balance between work and personal life is essential for our overall well-being. When we are constantly juggling multiple responsibilities, it's easy to feel overwhelmed and stressed. By adopting a more mindful approach to work and life, we can create a harmonious balance that allows us to thrive in both areas.

One of the first steps to achieving work-life balance is setting boundaries. This involves creating clear distinctions between work and personal time and sticking to them. Establish a designated workspace and set specific work hours, ensuring that you have time to relax and recharge. Communicate your boundaries to others, whether it's your boss, colleagues, or family members, so they understand and respect your needs.

Prioritizing self-care is also crucial for maintaining work-life balance. This means taking time for activities that nurture your physical, mental, and emotional well-being. Incorporate regular exercise, healthy eating, and sufficient sleep into your daily routine. Engage in activities that bring you joy and relaxation, such as hobbies, meditation, or spending time in nature. By prioritizing self-care, you can recharge your energy and approach your work and personal life with greater resilience.

Another key to balancing work and life is learning to delegate and ask for help. We often feel the need to do everything ourselves, but this can lead to burnout and decreased productivity. Identify tasks that can be delegated to others, whether it's at work or home, and don't be afraid to ask for assistance when needed. This not only reduces your workload but also empowers others and fosters a sense of collaboration and support.

Finally, practice mindfulness in both your work and personal life. When you are fully present and engaged in whatever you are doing, you can perform better and derive more satisfaction from your activities. Avoid multitasking and instead focus on one task at a time, giving it your full attention. This allows you to be more efficient and enjoy a greater sense of accomplishment. By integrating mindfulness into all aspects of your life, you can create a balanced and fulfilling existence.

5

Chapter 5: The Power of Positive Thinking

Positive thinking is a powerful tool that can transform our lives. By cultivating an optimistic mindset, we can navigate challenges with resilience, attract positive outcomes, and enhance our overall well-being. Adopting a positive outlook involves shifting our focus from what's wrong to what's right and embracing a mindset of possibility and growth.

One of the first steps to developing positive thinking is to become aware of our thoughts. Our minds are constantly filled with an internal dialogue that shapes our perception of the world. Pay attention to the nature of your thoughts and notice when they are negative or self-critical. Challenge these thoughts by questioning their validity and replacing them with more positive and empowering ones.

Another key aspect of positive thinking is practicing self-compassion. We are often our own harshest critics, and this can hinder our ability to stay positive. Treat yourself with the same kindness and understanding that you would offer a friend. Acknowledge your strengths and accomplishments, and be gentle with yourself when things don't go as planned. By practicing self-compassion, you can build a more positive and resilient mindset.

Gratitude is also a powerful practice for cultivating positive thinking. By focusing on the things we are grateful for, we can shift our attention away from what's lacking and appreciate the abundance in our lives. Make it a habit to regularly reflect on the things you are thankful for, whether it's through a gratitude journal or simply taking a moment each day to count your blessings. This practice can help to create a more positive and optimistic outlook.

Surrounding yourself with positive influences is also essential for maintaining a positive mindset. Seek out supportive and encouraging relationships, and distance yourself from negative influences that drain your energy. Engage in activities that uplift and inspire you, such as reading motivational books, listening to uplifting music, or engaging in hobbies that bring you joy. By surrounding yourself with positivity, you can create an environment that fosters a more optimistic and empowering outlook.

6

Chapter 6: Embracing Change and Adaptability

Change is an inevitable part of life, and our ability to adapt to new circumstances determines how well we navigate the twists and turns we encounter. Embracing change requires a mindset of flexibility and openness, allowing us to see opportunities even in the midst of challenges. By cultivating adaptability, we can thrive in a world that is constantly evolving.

One of the first steps to embracing change is to develop a growth mindset. This means viewing challenges as opportunities for learning and growth, rather than as obstacles to be feared. When we approach change with curiosity and a willingness to learn, we can discover new strengths and capabilities within ourselves. Practice reframing your thoughts about change, focusing on the potential benefits and growth that it can bring.

Another important aspect of adaptability is learning to let go of control. While it's natural to want to have a sense of control over our lives, the reality is that many things are beyond our control. Instead of resisting change, practice accepting it and finding ways to navigate it with grace. This involves being present in the moment and responding to new situations with a calm and open mind. By letting go of the need for control, we can approach change with greater ease and resilience.

Building a support network is also essential for navigating change. Surround yourself with people who can offer encouragement, guidance, and perspective during times of transition. This could be friends, family, colleagues, or mentors. Share your experiences and challenges with them, and be open to their advice and support. Having a strong support network can provide a sense of stability and reassurance, helping us to adapt more effectively to change.

Finally, practice self-care during times of change. Change can be stressful, and it's important to take care of our physical, mental, and emotional well-being. Make time for activities that help you relax and recharge, such as exercise, meditation, or spending time in nature. Be mindful of your needs and take steps to address them. By prioritizing self-care, we can maintain our resilience and navigate change with greater strength and positivity.

7

Chapter 7: Cultivating Creativity

Creativity is a powerful force that allows us to express ourselves, solve problems, and bring new ideas to life. By cultivating creativity, we can enrich our lives and tap into our full potential. Creativity is not limited to artistic pursuits; it can be applied to any area of life, from work to relationships to personal growth.

One of the first steps to cultivating creativity is to create an environment that fosters it. This involves setting aside time and space for creative activities and removing distractions that can hinder the creative process. Whether it's a dedicated workspace, a quiet corner of your home, or a regular time for creative pursuits, having a designated space and time for creativity can help to nurture and inspire new ideas.

Another important aspect of creativity is embracing curiosity and playfulness. Allow yourself to explore new ideas, experiment, and take risks. Approach challenges with a sense of curiosity and an open mind, and be willing to try new things. Playfulness can also spark creativity, so don't be afraid to have fun and enjoy the creative process. Engage in activities that inspire you, whether it's reading, listening to music, or spending time in nature, and let your imagination run wild.

Collaboration is also a key to fostering creativity. Engaging with others and sharing ideas can lead to new perspectives and innovative solutions. Seek out opportunities for collaboration, whether it's working on a project with colleagues, joining a creative group, or simply brainstorming with friends. Be open to feedback and new ideas, and be willing to learn from others. Collaboration can help to expand our creative horizons and inspire new possibilities.

Finally, practice mindfulness in your creative pursuits. Being fully present and engaged in the creative process allows us to tap into our intuition and inner wisdom. Practice mindfulness techniques, such as deep breathing or meditation, before starting a creative activity. Focus on the process rather than the outcome, and allow yourself to be in the moment. By integrating mindfulness into our creative practice, we can access deeper levels of creativity and bring our ideas to life with greater authenticity and originality.

8

Chapter 8: Building Resilience

Resilience is the ability to bounce back from adversity and overcome challenges. It is a vital quality that enables us to navigate life's ups and downs with strength and grace. By building resilience, we can face difficulties with greater confidence and emerge stronger from the experience.

One of the first steps to building resilience is to develop a positive mindset. This involves focusing on our strengths and capabilities, rather than dwelling on our limitations. Practice positive self-talk and remind yourself of past successes and achievements. By cultivating a positive mindset, we can approach challenges with greater optimism and determination.

Another important aspect of resilience is developing healthy coping strategies. This involves finding constructive ways to manage stress and emotions. Practice mindfulness techniques, such as meditation or deep breathing, to calm the mind and reduce stress. Engage in activities that bring you joy and relaxation, such as exercise, hobbies, or spending time with loved ones. Developing healthy coping strategies can help us to navigate challenges with greater ease and resilience.

Building strong relationships is also essential for resilience. Having a support network of friends, family, and colleagues can provide us with encouragement, guidance, and perspective during difficult times. Share your experiences and challenges with others, and be open to their advice and support. Building strong relationships can provide a sense of stability and reassurance, helping us to overcome adversity.

Finally, practice self-care to maintain your resilience. This involves taking care of your physical, mental, and emotional well-being. Make time for activities that help you relax and recharge, such as exercise, meditation, or spending time in nature. Be mindful of your needs and take steps to address them. By prioritizing self-care, we can maintain our resilience and navigate life's challenges with greater strength and positivity.

9

Chapter 9: Enhancing Emotional Intelligence

Emotional intelligence is the ability to understand and manage our own emotions, as well as the emotions of others. It is a crucial skill that enables us to build strong relationships, navigate social interactions, and make informed decisions. By enhancing our emotional intelligence, we can improve our well-being and achieve greater success in our personal and professional lives.

One of the first steps to enhancing emotional intelligence is to develop self-awareness. This involves understanding our own emotions and how they influence our thoughts and behaviors. Practice mindfulness techniques, such as meditation or journaling, to increase your awareness of your emotions. Pay attention to how you feel in different situations and notice any patterns or triggers. By developing self-awareness, we can better understand our emotions and respond to them in a constructive way.

Another important aspect of emotional intelligence is self-regulation. This involves managing our emotions and behaviors in a way that is appropriate and constructive. Practice techniques such as deep breathing or counting to ten to calm yourself in stressful situations. Develop healthy coping strategies for managing difficult emotions, such as talking to a friend, exercising, or engaging in a creative activity. By practicing self-regulation, we can maintain our composure and respond to challenges with greater resilience.

Empathy is also a key component of emotional intelligence. This involves understanding and being sensitive to the emotions of others. Practice active listening and pay attention to the feelings and perspectives of those around you. Show compassion and understanding in your interactions, and be mindful of how your words and actions may impact others. By cultivating empathy, we can build stronger relationships and foster a greater sense of connection and understanding.

Finally, practice effective communication to enhance your emotional intelligence. This involves expressing your thoughts and feelings clearly and constructively, as well as listening actively and empathetically to others. Practice assertive communication, where you express your needs and boundaries in a respectful and confident manner. Be open to feedback and willing to adjust your communication style as needed. By practicing effective communication, we can navigate social interactions with greater ease and build more meaningful connections.

10

Chapter 10: Practicing Mindful Eating

Mindful eating is the practice of paying full attention to the experience of eating and drinking. It involves savoring each bite, being aware of the flavors, textures, and aromas, and tuning into our body's hunger and fullness signals. By practicing mindful eating, we can develop a healthier relationship with food and enhance our overall well-being.

One of the first steps to practicing mindful eating is to create a calm and distraction-free environment. Sit down at a table, turn off the TV, and put away your phone. Take a few deep breaths to center yourself and focus on the meal in front of you. This helps to create a sense of mindfulness and allows you to fully engage with the eating experience.

Another important aspect of mindful eating is to eat slowly and savor each bite. Take small bites and chew thoroughly, paying attention to the flavors, textures, and sensations in your mouth. This not only enhances the enjoyment of the meal but also allows your body to properly digest the food and recognize when it is full. Put your fork down between bites and take your time to fully experience each mouthful.

Listening to your body's hunger and fullness signals is also crucial for mindful eating. Pay attention to how your body feels before, during, and after eating. Notice when you start to feel hungry and when you begin to feel full. Eat when you are hungry and stop when you are satisfied, rather than when you are stuffed. By tuning into your body's signals, you can develop a healthier and more balanced approach to eating.

Finally, practice gratitude and appreciation for your food. Take a moment before eating to express gratitude for the meal in front of you and the effort that went into preparing it. Appreciate the colors, smells, and flavors of the food, and recognize the nourishment it provides to your body. By practicing gratitude, we can cultivate a deeper connection to our food and enhance the overall eating experience.

11

Chapter 11: Managing Stress and Anxiety

Stress and anxiety are common challenges that many of us face in our daily lives. Managing these feelings is essential for our overall well-being and mental health. By adopting a mindful approach to stress and anxiety, we can develop healthier coping strategies and navigate these challenges with greater resilience.

One of the first steps to managing stress and anxiety is to identify the sources of these feelings. Pay attention to the situations, thoughts, and behaviors that trigger stress and anxiety. By understanding the root causes, we can develop more effective strategies for managing them. Keep a journal to track your triggers and explore potential solutions.

Another important aspect of managing stress and anxiety is to practice mindfulness techniques. Mindfulness involves being fully present in the moment and observing our thoughts and feelings without judgment. Practice mindfulness meditation, deep breathing exercises, or progressive muscle relaxation to calm the mind and reduce stress. These techniques can help to create a sense of inner peace and resilience.

Developing healthy lifestyle habits is also crucial for managing stress and anxiety. This includes regular exercise, a balanced diet, and sufficient sleep. Engage in physical activities that you enjoy, such as walking, yoga, or dancing, to release tension and boost your mood. Eat a nutritious diet that supports your overall health, and prioritize quality sleep to recharge your body and mind.

Lastly, seek support when needed. Reach out to friends, family, or a mental health professional for support and guidance. Talking about your feelings and experiences can provide a sense of relief and perspective. Join a support group or community that shares similar challenges, and be open to receiving help. By seeking support, we can navigate stress and anxiety with greater strength and resilience.

12

Chapter 12: Developing a Growth Mindset

A growth mindset is the belief that our abilities and intelligence can be developed through effort, learning, and perseverance. This mindset allows us to embrace challenges, learn from failures, and achieve greater success in our personal and professional lives. By developing a growth mindset, we can unlock our full potential and create a more fulfilling and rewarding life.

One of the first steps to developing a growth mindset is to embrace challenges and view them as opportunities for growth. When faced with a difficult task or situation, approach it with curiosity and a willingness to learn. Recognize that challenges are a natural part of the learning process and an opportunity to develop new skills and knowledge. By embracing challenges, we can build resilience and confidence in our abilities.

Another important aspect of a growth mindset is to learn from failures and setbacks. Instead of viewing failures as a reflection of our abilities, see them as valuable learning experiences. Reflect on what went wrong, what you can learn from the experience, and how you can improve in the future. By viewing failures as opportunities for growth, we can develop a more resilient and adaptive mindset.

Cultivating a love for learning is also essential for a growth mindset.

Develop a passion for continuous learning and seek out opportunities for personal and professional development. Read books, take courses, attend workshops, and engage in activities that challenge and inspire you. By fostering a love for learning, we can stay motivated and curious, and continuously expand our knowledge and skills.

Finally, practice positive self-talk and believe in your ability to grow and improve. Replace negative thoughts and self-doubt with positive affirmations and encouragement. Remind yourself of your strengths and achievements, and celebrate your progress, no matter how small. By cultivating a positive and empowering mindset, we can overcome obstacles and achieve our goals.

13

Chapter 13: Enhancing Focus and Concentration

Focus and concentration are essential for achieving our goals and performing at our best. In today's fast-paced world, it's easy to become distracted and lose focus. By adopting mindful practices and strategies, we can enhance our focus and concentration, and achieve greater productivity and success.

One of the first steps to enhancing focus and concentration is to create a conducive environment. This involves eliminating distractions and setting up a workspace that supports concentration. Remove clutter, turn off notifications, and create a quiet and comfortable space for work or study. A well-organized and distraction-free environment can help to improve focus and productivity.

Another important aspect of enhancing focus is to practice mindfulness techniques. Mindfulness involves being fully present in the moment and paying attention to our thoughts and sensations. Practice mindfulness meditation, deep breathing exercises, or body scans to calm the mind and improve concentration. These techniques can help to reduce stress and increase our ability to stay focused.

Setting clear goals and priorities is also crucial for maintaining focus. Break down larger tasks into smaller, manageable steps and set specific deadlines for each step. Use tools such as to-do lists, calendars, or project management apps to stay organized and on track. By setting clear goals and priorities, we can stay focused on what matters most and avoid getting overwhelmed.

Finally, take regular breaks to recharge and avoid burnout. While it may seem counterintuitive, taking breaks can actually improve focus and productivity. Schedule short breaks throughout the day to rest and rejuvenate. Engage in activities that help you relax and recharge, such as stretching, walking, or listening to music. By taking care of our well-being, we can maintain our focus and perform at our best.

14

Chapter 14: Building Strong Support Networks

Support networks play a crucial role in our well-being and success. They provide us with encouragement, guidance, and a sense of belonging. By building strong support networks, we can navigate challenges more effectively and achieve our goals with greater confidence and resilience.

One of the first steps to building a strong support network is to cultivate meaningful relationships. This involves being open and authentic in our interactions with others. Take the time to get to know people on a deeper level and share your thoughts and feelings honestly. Practice active listening and show empathy and understanding in your interactions. By building trust and mutual respect, we can create strong and supportive relationships.

Another important aspect of building a support network is to seek out diverse connections. Surround yourself with people from different backgrounds, experiences, and perspectives. This diversity can provide you with a broader range of insights and support. Join clubs, organizations, or communities that align with your interests and values, and be open to meeting new people. By expanding your social network, you can access a wider range of resources and support.

Offering support to others is also essential for building strong support networks. Be there for your friends, family, and colleagues when they need help, and offer your assistance and encouragement. Practice acts of kindness and generosity, and be willing to lend a listening ear or a helping hand. By supporting others, we can strengthen our relationships and create a sense of reciprocity and trust.

Finally, practice gratitude and appreciation for the support you receive. Acknowledge and thank those who have been there for you, and express your appreciation for their efforts and support. This not only strengthens your relationships but also reinforces the positive behaviors and qualities that contribute to a strong support network. By practicing gratitude, we can create a more supportive and connected community.

15

Chapter 15: Developing Time Management Skills

Effective time management is essential for achieving our goals and maintaining a balanced and fulfilling life. By developing time management skills, we can make the most of our time and accomplish more with less stress. This involves prioritizing tasks, setting goals, and staying organized and focused.

One of the first steps to effective time management is to set clear and achievable goals. Break down larger projects into smaller, manageable tasks and set specific deadlines for each step. Use tools such as to-do lists, calendars, and project management apps to stay organized and on track. By setting clear goals and priorities, we can stay focused on what matters most and avoid getting overwhelmed.

Another important aspect of time management is to create a daily routine. Routines provide structure and predictability, helping us to stay organized and focused. Start by creating a morning routine that sets a positive tone for the day, and follow it with a consistent schedule for work and personal activities. Include regular breaks to recharge and avoid burnout. A well-planned routine allows us to manage our time more efficiently and accomplish more with less effort.

Eliminating distractions is also crucial for effective time management.

Identify the factors that disrupt your focus and find ways to minimize or eliminate them. This may involve creating a dedicated workspace, turning off notifications, or setting boundaries with others. Practice single-tasking, where you focus on one task at a time, rather than multitasking. By reducing distractions and maintaining focus, you can work more efficiently and produce higher-quality results.

Finally, practice self-discipline and accountability in your time management. Set clear boundaries and stick to them, and hold yourself accountable for meeting your goals and deadlines. Use techniques such as time blocking or the Pomodoro Technique to stay focused and productive. By practicing self-discipline and accountability, we can develop more effective time management skills and achieve greater success in our personal and professional lives.

16

Chapter 16: Exploring Mindful Movement

Mindful movement involves being fully present and aware during physical activities. This practice can enhance our physical health, reduce stress, and promote a sense of well-being. By incorporating mindful movement into our daily routines, we can cultivate a deeper connection to our bodies and enhance our overall quality of life.

One of the first steps to practicing mindful movement is to choose activities that you enjoy and that align with your fitness level and goals. This could be anything from yoga and tai chi to walking, dancing, or swimming. The key is to find activities that you find enjoyable and that allow you to move mindfully and with awareness.

Another important aspect of mindful movement is to focus on the sensations in your body as you move. Pay attention to your breath, the feeling of your muscles working, and the rhythm of your movements. Practice moving slowly and deliberately, and be mindful of your posture and alignment. This awareness can help to improve your physical performance and reduce the risk of injury.

Incorporating mindfulness techniques into your movement practice can also enhance the experience. Practice deep breathing, meditation, or visualization before, during, or after your physical activities. Use these techniques to calm the mind, reduce stress, and enhance your overall sense of well-being. By integrating mindfulness into your movement practice, you can create a more holistic and balanced approach to physical fitness.

Finally, practice gratitude and appreciation for your body and its capabilities. Acknowledge the strength, flexibility, and resilience of your body, and express gratitude for the ability to move and engage in physical activities. This practice can help to cultivate a positive and empowering relationship with your body and enhance your overall sense of well-being.

17

Chapter 17: Creating a Mindful Home Environment

Our home environment plays a significant role in our well-being and happiness. By creating a mindful and nurturing home environment, we can promote a sense of peace, relaxation, and well-being. This involves creating a space that reflects our values and supports our physical, mental, and emotional health.

One of the first steps to creating a mindful home environment is to declutter and organize your space. Remove unnecessary items and create a clean and organized environment. This can help to reduce stress and create a sense of calm and order. Use storage solutions, such as baskets, shelves, and containers, to keep your space organized and tidy.

Another important aspect of a mindful home environment is to incorporate elements that promote relaxation and well-being. This could include plants, natural light, soothing colors, and comfortable furnishings. Create spaces that encourage relaxation and mindfulness, such as a meditation corner, a reading nook, or a cozy spot for reflection. By incorporating elements that promote well-being, we can create a more nurturing and supportive home environment.

Incorporating mindfulness practices into your daily home routines can also enhance the overall environment. Practice mindfulness techniques, such as deep breathing, meditation, or gratitude exercises, as part of your daily routine. Create rituals and habits that promote mindfulness and well-being, such as enjoying a cup of tea mindfully, spending time in nature, or engaging in creative activities. By integrating mindfulness into our home life, we can create a more peaceful and harmonious environment.

Finally, practice gratitude and appreciation for your home and the environment it provides. Acknowledge the comfort, safety, and support that your home offers, and express gratitude for the space you live in. This practice can help to cultivate a deeper connection to your home and enhance your overall sense of well-being.

Threaded Days: Weaving Mindfulness, Productivity, and Relationships into Everyday Life

In the hustle and bustle of modern life, finding a sense of balance and fulfillment can often feel like an elusive dream. "Threaded Days" offers a transformative guide to weaving mindfulness, productivity, and meaningful relationships into the fabric of your everyday life. This insightful book takes you on a journey of self-discovery and growth, empowering you to live with intention, clarity, and connection.

Through seventeen thoughtfully crafted chapters, you will explore the art of mindful living, discovering practical techniques to stay present and fully engaged in each moment. Learn how to cultivate productive habits that prioritize what truly matters, allowing you to achieve your goals without sacrificing your well-being. Dive into the realm of relationships, uncovering the secrets to building strong, supportive connections that enrich your life.

"Threaded Days" also delves into essential topics such as embracing change, developing a growth mindset, and enhancing emotional intelligence. With practical advice and relatable anecdotes, this book provides you with the tools to navigate life's challenges with grace and resilience. Whether you are seeking to enhance your focus, manage stress, or create a nurturing home environment, "Threaded Days" offers a comprehensive and holistic approach to living a balanced and fulfilling life.

Embrace the journey of weaving mindfulness, productivity, and relationships into the tapestry of your daily existence. Let "Threaded Days" be your

CHAPTER 17: CREATING A MINDFUL HOME ENVIRONMENT

guide to creating a life that is not only successful but also deeply meaningful and connected.

www.ingramcontent.com/pod-product-compliance
Lightning Source LLC
LaVergne TN
LVHW020500080526
838202LV00057B/6061